# The Space

## Sheila Lane and Marion Kemp

CAMBRIDGE UNIVERSITY PRESS
Cambridge
London   New York   New Rochelle
Melbourne   Sydney

# The Space Machine

A group of children, playing on some waste ground, find an old metal box. They realise that it is some kind of Space Machine when they hear strange voices coming from it. The Space Machine has a panel like a television screen, and as they are investigating it, a picture appears. The picture shows a group of robots on a far away planet; the events on this planet, watched by the children, are told as the first play. When that story is finished the Space Machine sends pictures from two more planets, and the next two plays are about the characters and happenings the children watch on these two planets.

After the scenes have faded away the children decide to take their Space Machine to the Space Society for universal use.

The children who find the Space Machine are the **Playwatchers.** The characters who take part in the plays on the three planets are the **Playmakers.**

# Contents

| | |
|---|---|
| Playwatchers | page 6 |
| **PLANET CHANGA** | 10 |
| Playwatchers | 27 |
| **PLANET STRATA** | 30 |
| Playwatchers | 49 |
| **PLANET CRYSTA** | 51 |
| Playwatchers | 67 |
| Suggestions for the Playmakers | 69 |

 # PLAYWATCHERS

JOSIE  
KAM  ] three children who are playing on some empty ground near a dump  
SANDY

---

*The arena is set up with a pile of boxes at the back.* JOSIE *runs in and looks for a hiding place.*

KAM, SANDY  (*call from off stage*)
Josie! Josie! Give us a call!
A shout or a whistle, or nothing at all!

(JOSIE *goes behind the boxes and whistles.* KAM *and* SANDY *run in.*)

KAM  Come on! (*pointing*) Over there!

SANDY  I can hear breathing!

(*Both rush to boxes.*)

KAM  Got you, Josie!

SANDY  (*looking at wrist watch*) That was ... ONE MINUTE ... TWENTY SECONDS! (*looking at Josie*) What's the matter?

JOSIE  Listen! I can hear something. It's coming from one of these old boxes ... It's the metal one.

(*All listen.*)

KAM  I can't hear anything.

SANDY  Nor me! It's probably your heart beating, Josie.

JOSIE  No it's not!

KAM  (*laughing*) Of course it is!

| | |
|---|---|
| SANDY | You'd be dead if it wasn't! |
| JOSIE | It's not my heart. Look! It's . . . THIS! |
| KAM | What is it? |
| SANDY | It's some kind of radio. |
| KAM | Or television set. |
| SANDY | There is something . . . LISTEN! |

(*All listen.*)

| | |
|---|---|
| KAM | Let's take it out and look properly. |

(*They pull out the metal box.*)

| | |
|---|---|
| SANDY | Perhaps it's a U.F.O. . . . you know . . . AN UNIDENTIFIED FLYING OBJECT. |
| JOSIE | Or a Space Machine! Watch me! I'm off to explore the universe! (*pulling lever*) |

(*A light comes on. Loud ticking is heard. All three children step back in amazement.*)

| | |
|---|---|
| KAM | It's alive! |
| JOSIE | I told you! It's some kind of Space Machine. I'm not joking, you know. I mean it. |
| KAM | It will probably fade out in a minute. |
| SANDY | When the battery runs flat! |
| JOSIE | (*seriously*) It can't run flat . . . It's powered by universal electricity! |
| KAM | What's that? |

| | |
|---|---|
| SANDY | Josie's always having mad ideas. Take no notice! |
| JOSIE | I'm off to space, you know! Watch me go! Wheeee . . . |
| KAM | Pull that top lever . . . and I'll come with you. |
| SANDY | Don't leave me behind. I know! I'll pull it too. Let's do it together. |
| ALL CHILDREN | One . . . two . . . three . . . PULL! (*They pull lever. Loud crackly voice sounds.*) |
| JOSIE | (*excitedly*) It's a voice! It's a voice! |
| KAM | Slow it down so that we can hear what it says. |
| JOSIE | I can't! There's nothing on it for altering the speed. |
| SANDY | Say something to it, then. |
| JOSIE | (*loudly*) WHO ARE YOU? (*banging on box*) WHO ARE YOU AND WHERE DO YOU COME FROM? |
| VOICES | (*clearly*) WHO ARE YOU AND WHERE DO YOU COME FROM? |
| KAM | (*sounding disappointed*) Those are the words Josie said. |
| SANDY | It's just some kind of echo. |
| JOSIE | No! There were lots of voices. Listen! |
| KAM | Look! It's lighting up! |

| | |
|---:|:---|
| SANDY | (*pointing*) It's got a kind of . . . screen. |
| ALL CHILDREN | **LOOK! SPACE MEN!** |
| JOSIE | Let's watch! |
| | (*Light fades on children.*) |

*Here begins the story of* **Planet Changa.**

# Planet Changa

## Playmakers

**Changans** – a race of masked robots, inhabiting Planet Changa
GREAT CHANG
CHANGA ONE
CHANGA TWO
CHANGAN GUARDS (four or more)

**Zarans** – humanoids from Planet Zara
KAL
NOVA ⎤ Zaran scouts

COMMANDER of Zarans
ROMA
KY ⎤ his lieutenants

ZAR ONE
ZAR TWO

FIRST COMMANDO
SECOND COMMANDO
THIRD COMMANDO
FOURTH COMMANDO

# Planet Changa

*The arena lights up.* CHANGA ONE *and* CHANGA TWO *are questioning the Zaran prisoners,* KAL *and* NOVA, *who are held by the* GUARDS. *The Changans speak in slow and monotonous voices.*

| | |
|---|---|
| CHANGA ONE | Who are you? |
| CHANGA TWO | And where do you come from? |
| ALL CHANGANS | Who are you and where do you come from? |
| KAL | We're Zarans. Look! (*pointing to sign on tunic*) Here is our sign. |
| CHANGA ONE | We do not know signs. What are you doing on Planet Changa? |
| NOVA | Exploring! Look! (*showing papers*) Here are our papers. |
| CHANGA TWO | We do not know papers. How have you come to Planet Changa? |
| KAL | We came in our space craft – Explorer Zero Five. |
| NOVA | Now tell us something. Are you the robots of Changa? |
| CHANGA ONE | We do not answer questions. |
| CHANGA TWO | We ask them. |
| KAL | (*to Nova*) Just as we thought! |
| NOVA | (*nodding*) They talk like machines! |
| KAL | (*to Changans*) Take us to someone who DOES answer questions. |
| NOVA | We know that you have a leader with a thinking brain. Take us to your leader. |
| CHANGA ONE | Our leader comes! |
| | (*Enter* GREAT CHANG.) |

| | |
|---|---|
| CHANGA TWO | Hail to our leader! |
| ALL CHANGANS | Our leader comes! Hail to our leader! Hail to the Great Chang! |

(KAL *and* NOVA *begin to move forward.*)

| | |
|---|---|
| CHANGA ONE | Do not move! |
| CHANGA TWO | Or you will be exterminated! |
| ALL CHANGANS | **DO NOT MOVE OR YOU WILL BE EXTERMINATED!** |
| GREAT CHANG | Who are your prisoners? |
| CHANGA ONE | They say they are Zarans, Great Chang. |
| GREAT CHANG | Humanoids! Zarans are humanoids. (*to Kal and Nova*) Why have you come to Planet Changa, Zarans? |
| KAL | We are explorers, Great Chang. |
| NOVA | Explorers and map makers. |
| KAL | We are on a great voyage of space exploration. |
| NOVA | We are searching the universe for new planets. |
| KAL | When we find a new planet, we chart it on our maps. |
| NOVA | We came to the unknown planet of Changa to ... |
| GREAT CHANG | (*holding up hand*) Correction! You say UNKNOWN! If Planet Changa was unknown, how did you know it was here? |
| KAL | (*to Nova*) Good thinking! |
| NOVA | (*nodding*) This must be the one with the thinking brain. |
| GREAT CHANG | Changans! Give First Warning. |
| CHANGA ONE | (*to Zarans*) Do not speak to each other! |
| CHANGA TWO | Or you will be exterminated! |

| | |
|---|---|
| ALL CHANGANS | **DO NOT SPEAK TO EACH OTHER OR YOU WILL BE EXTERMINATED!** |
| KAL | Sorry! |
| NOVA | We were just admiring your thinking brain, Great Chang. |
| GREAT CHANG | How did you come here, Zarans? |
| KAL | In our space craft, Explorer Zero Five. |
| GREAT CHANG | Where is the space craft now? |
| NOVA | On the other side of the Sea of Rocks. |
| GREAT CHANG | If you came to Planet Changa in a space craft, you did not come alone. Where are your friends? |
| KAL | Good thinking Great Chang! The others are . . . (*shrugging shoulders*) somewhere. |
| NOVA | (*shrugging*) . . . somewhere around! |
| GREAT CHANG | You answer in a careless manner, Zarans. Changans! Give Second Warning. |
| CHANGA ONE | Do not answer in a careless manner! |
| CHANGA TWO | Or you will be exterminated! |
| ALL CHANGANS | **DO NOT ANSWER IN A CARELESS MANNER OR YOU WILL BE EXTERMINATED!** |
| KAL | Sorry . . . again! |
| NOVA | We must be careful, Kal! |
| GREAT CHANG | (*to Changa One*) What weapons did these Zarans carry? |
| CHANGA ONE | (*nervously*) We have not . . . We have not . . . We have not . . . |
| GREAT CHANG | (*to Changa One*) If you have failed to carry out the correct operations, you will be punished. Scan the prisoners for weapons. |

|   |   |
|---|---|
| | (CHANGA ONE *and* CHANGA TWO *pass scanners over prisoners.*) |
| CHANGA ONE | No weapons! |
| CHANGA TWO | The prisoners have no weapons. |
| KAL | We're here on a peaceful mission, Great Chang. |
| NOVA | We're searching for new planets. That's the truth. |
| GREAT CHANG | TRUTH! We shall soon know. (*to Changa One*) Put the prisoners on the truth machine. |
| | (*The truth machine (see p. 72) is pulled forward. The hands of Kal and Nova are put onto its handles.*) |
| GREAT CHANG | Give your names. |
| KAL | Kal! |
| NOVA | Nova! |
| GREAT CHANG | Answer all questions with truth, or you will be punished. Who are your people? |
| KAL AND NOVA | Our people are Zarans. |
| ALL CHANGANS | The truth machine says TRUTHFUL ANSWER. |
| GREAT CHANG | Where is your space craft? |
| KAL AND NOVA | Our space craft is one point five miles north of the Sea of Rocks. |
| ALL CHANGANS | The truth machine says TRUTHFUL ANSWER. |
| GREAT CHANG | How many Zarans have come to Changa? |
| KAL AND NOVA | Eleven Zarans have come to Changa. |
| ALL CHANGANS | The truth machine says TRUTHFUL ANSWER. |
| GREAT CHANG | So! There are eleven Zarans on Planet Changa. (*louder*) You are SPIES! True or false? |
| KAL AND NOVA | False! |
| GREAT CHANG | You are searching Planet Changa for precious jewels and stones. True or false? |
| KAL AND NOVA | False! |

| | |
|---|---|
| GREAT CHANG | You have come to Planet Changa to steal our new inventions. True or false? |
| KAL AND NOVA | False! |
| GREAT CHANG | Changans! What does the truth machine say? |
| ALL CHANGANS | The truth machine says, ALL ANSWERS TRUTHFUL. |
| GREAT CHANG | The truth machine cannot lie. Release the Zarans from the machine. |

(KAL *and* NOVA *look relieved as they are taken from the truth machine.*)

| | |
|---|---|
| KAL | It is all as we said, Great Chang. |
| NOVA | May we go free now and explore the planet? |
| GREAT CHANG | FREE! We do not know the word FREE on Planet Changa. |
| KAL | But we told the truth. |
| NOVA | The machine said that all our answers were truthful. |
| GREAT CHANG | So! You may live! |
| KAL | But we cannot live here, Great Chang. |
| NOVA | We are Zaran explorers. We cannot live here on Planet Changa. |
| GREAT CHANG | You came here! You must live here! You must work here! |
| KAL AND NOVA | WORK! |
| GREAT CHANG | All who come here must work. (*to guards*) Take the Zarans to the work unit. |
| KAL | (*imploringly*) Great Chang! We are Zarans! |
| NOVA | We came here peacefully . . . We came to explore . . . Let us . . . |

| | |
|---|---|
| GREAT CHANG | (*interrupting*) Put the Zarans in Work Unit Four. |
| ALL GUARDS | We will put the Zarans in Work Unit Four, Great Chang. |

(KAL *and* NOVA *are taken away roughly by Changan* GUARDS.)

| | |
|---|---|
| GREAT CHANG | Changa One! |
| CHANGA ONE | I hear and obey, Great Chang. |
| GREAT CHANG | You failed to scan the prisoners for weapons. |
| CHANGA ONE | I failed to scan the prisoners for weapons. |
| GREAT CHANG | You will lose your position as chief guard and return to the work unit. Do you understand? |
| CHANGA ONE | I understand and obey, Great Chang. (*He takes off his chief guard badge and goes out.*) |
| GREAT CHANG | (*to Changa Two*) You will be tried as chief guard. But make no mistakes or you will return to the work unit also. Do you understand? |
| CHANGA TWO | (*taking chief guard badge*) I understand and obey. |

(GREAT CHANG *goes out.*)

I must make no mistakes or I will return to the work unit.

(*As Changa Two pins badge on tunic, two Zarans creep up behind him.* ZAR ONE *puts one hand over Changa Two's mouth and uses other hand to pin his hands.* ZAR TWO *bumps Changa Two's head with stun ball.*)

| | |
|---|---|
| ZAR ONE | Don't bother with the badge, comrade! |
| ZAR TWO | You've come to the end of your short working life as chief guard. (*He ties hands of unconscious Changan.*) |
| ZAR ONE | Sweet dreams . . . if robots dream! |

| | |
|---|---|
| ZAR TWO | (*beckons and calls*) Over here, commander! Come over here! |
| | (ZARAN COMMANDER *enters, with* ROMA *and* KY.) |
| COMMANDER | That makes the score two to one. |
| ZAR ONE | But it's two to them! |
| ZAR TWO | And only one to us. (*pointing to Changan on ground*) This one! |
| ROMA | We can thank our lucky stars that we saw what was happening on the commander's built-in glove television set. |
| KY | The Changans have got both our scouts. So, now what do we do? |
| COMMANDER | Think of a way to get them back. |
| ALL | How? |
| COMMANDER | Use this! (*tapping forehead*) This is where we have the advantage over all the robots in the universe. |
| ROMA | Haven't these robot Changans any brains at all? |
| KY | Great Chang has! Don't you agree, commander? |
| COMMANDER | Our Advance Information System described Great Chang as the program setter. This means that he can make all the others do what he wants. |
| ROMA | But what about his brain? |
| KY | Is it able to work . . . like ours? |
| COMMANDER | I doubt it! We humanoids have real brains . . . real think-tanks . . . which we can use to make our plans. But even more important, we can use our brains to change those plans according to circumstances. |
| ROMA | That's true! When things go wrong, we can just change our program and try something else. |

KY — Can't these robots change their program at all, commander? I mean ... if they're going in the wrong direction, do they have to go on?

COMMANDER — Something like that! But remember that the Changans are led by Great Chang. Ky saw that he was different ... I'm not sure how. But he's got some brain power. (*thoughtfully*) Don't ask me how he makes it work.

ROMA — Work! Ah! WORK UNIT! The Changans have taken Kal and Nova to their work unit.

KY — So what shall we do?

ZAR ONE — Get them out.

ZAR TWO — We've got our ray guns.

ZAR ONE — Those robots won't be able to stand up to Zaran ray guns.

ZAR TWO — Let's blast our way into the work unit.

COMMANDER — Wait! Listen, Zarans! Never, never, never believe that you are dealing with a powerless enemy! These Changans have their own kind of power and Great Chang has a brain ... of a kind. Besides, our Advance Information System described them as being very clever with weapons.

ROMA — So, if their programs were set correctly, they could mow us down.

KY — Mow us down! Ugh! We need six Zarans to fly the space craft.

COMMANDER — There are four commando Zarans guarding the craft. But that's not the point. We can't leave Kal and Nova in a Changan work unit, so ...

ROMA — Click! Click! Click! What's your think-tank doing, commander?

| | |
|---|---|
| COMMANDER | Working overtime! Zar One! Zar Two! Get that Changan's tunic and face mask. I'm going to need them. |
| KY | So . . . you're going in . . . in disguise. |
| COMMANDER | That's the idea. |
| ROMA | It's risky, commander. |
| COMMANDER | Sure! So we'll risk just one of us . . . ME! |
| ZAR ONE | Here's the mask. |
| COMMANDER | (*holding mask up to face*) How do I look? |
| KY | Much better! (*All laugh.*) |
| COMMANDER | (*jokingly*) Zarans! I give you First Warning! Do not make jokes about your commander . . . or you will be exterminated! |
| ROMA | Keep your humanoid brain, commander! You're going to need it. |
| ZAR TWO | Here's the tunic, commander. |
| COMMANDER | (*slipping tunic over his own clothing*) It's not a complete disguise, but it will fool anyone who takes a quick look. |
| ZAR ONE | Your legs and boots are Zaran. |
| COMMANDER | (*looking down at legs*) They're not so very different. Most people see what they expect to see . . . especially robots! |
| KY | Just keep one hand on your ray gun, that's all. |
| COMMANDER | Don't worry! My plan is to get in there, and then . . . head up . . . quick march . . . straight past any Changans I meet. |
| ROMA | Suppose you are challenged? |
| COMMANDER | (*laughing*) I shall have to change my program! (*seriously*) I don't think I shall be. After all, the |

| | |
|---|---|
| COMMANDER cont. | Changans are expecting to see this fellow (*pointing to unconscious Changan*) proving himself as chief guard. |
| KY | I wish you were leaving us your glove television, commander, so that we could see what's going on. |
| COMMANDER | No chance! I'm the one who needs to know where everyone is. Look! |

(*All crowd round glove television.*)

They haven't taken Kal and Nova far. (*pointing to television*) That must be a work unit.

| | |
|---|---|
| ZAR TWO | They both look fine. But hang on to your ray gun, commander. |
| ROMA | And your glove television. |
| COMMANDER | Sure! And remember, I can use my strongest weapon of all! (*tapping forehead*) This! |
| ALL | (*tapping foreheads*) Our humanoid think-tanks! |
| COMMANDER | (*pulling down mask*) O.K. Changans! Here I come! (*He marches out.*) |
| ZAR ONE | What do you think his chances are, Ky? |
| KY | Pretty good, knowing the commander. |
| ZAR TWO | I wish we could do something. |
| ZAR ONE | This waiting makes me jumpy. |
| ZAR TWO | Listen! What was that? |
| ROMA | ALERT! (*All stand still.*) SCAN! (*All look round.*) |
| KY | False alarm! Sound travels quickly on Changa. I've noticed that. |
| ROMA | I hope the space craft's O.K. The commandos will be keeping contact with us, but we've no way of knowing if they're all right. |

| | |
|---|---|
| KY | Let's hope the Changan's haven't set their program to 'LET'S INVESTIGATE SPACE CRAFT'. |
| ROMA | That space craft is our life-line . . . to Zara. |
| ZAR ONE | I heard a footstep then. |
| ZAR TWO | Over there! (*pointing*) |
| ROMA | ALERT! (*All stand still.*)<br>SCAN! (*All look round.*)<br>HOLD ALERT! (*Footsteps are heard.*)<br>HANDS ON RAY GUNS! (*All put their left hands into tunic pockets.*)<br>STUN BALLS READY! (*All raise stun balls in right hands.*)<br>(*Enter* COMMANDER *marching* KAL *and* NOVA *in front of him.*) |
| ZAR ONE | (*in astonishment*) Quick work! |
| ZAR TWO | However did . . .? |
| COMMANDER | (*interrupting*) No explanations, Zarans! We're not safe yet. Wait until we get back to the craft. |
| ROMA | I hope it's O.K. |
| COMMANDER | Just get back to it! (*pointing to unconscious Changan*) That stun ball won't keep him in the land of dreams for ever. |
| KY | We'll wait . . . |
| COMMANDER | No! Someone in there (*pointing to work unit*) will soon register that Kal and Nova are missing. There's no time to be lost. |
| ROMA | What's the idea, commander? |
| COMMANDER | You get Explorer Zero Five ready for take-off and I'll think of some delaying tactics. |

(*All* ZARANS *hurry out.*)

| | |
|---|---|
| KY | (*calls back*) Don't wait too long. |
| COMMANDER | (*bending over Changan*) I'll put this mask back on the Changan. I'll make him look . . . normal . . . That's better. Now the tunic . . . GOOD! |
| | (COMMANDER *moves quickly to side as* GREAT CHANG *strides in. He sees Changan lying on ground.*) |
| GREAT CHANG | Chief guard! (*looking round*) Where are the Zarans? (*bending over Changan and thumping his chest*) Out of action! (*He pulls cords from Changan's hands.*) I must call EMERGENCY! (*He begins to stand up.*) |
| COMMANDER | (*lunging forward and grasping Great Chang's arm*) Oh no, Great Chang! We won't have you calling in your emergency services yet . . . |
| GREAT CHANG | HUMANOID! |
| COMMANDER | . . . or your little robot army. |
| GREAT CHANG | (*raising other arm*) We'll . . . SEE! |
| | (CHANGA TWO *slowly pulls himself upright.*) |
| | No-one can escape from the Great Chang. |
| COMMANDER | I shouldn't count on it, Chang! |
| | (CHANGA TWO *staggers forward and pulls Commander's arm from Great Chang's.*) |
| GREAT CHANG | (*beating chest and calling loudly*) CHANG! CHANG! CHANG! |
| | (ALL CHANGANS *rush in and hold commander.*) |
| | Do not move, humanoid! |
| ALL CHANGANS | DO NOT MOVE OR YOU WILL BE EXTERMINATED! |
| GREAT CHANG | So! You thought you could escape from the Great Chang, humanoid. |

| | |
|---|---|
| COMMANDER | You win this round, Chang! |
| GREAT CHANG | Great Chang wins . . . all . . . ROUNDS! |
| COMMANDER | (*holding up hands*) As I said . . . YOU WIN . . . (*He quickly drops hand and twists left glove round.*) . . . THIS ROUND! |
| GREAT CHANG | (*shouts*) THE HUMANOID'S HAND! IT IS A SECRET WEAPON! GET IT! |
| COMMANDER | You can't have my hand without me, Chang! (*He moves forward.*) |
| GREAT CHANG | Hold the humanoid! He has a secret weapon! Get it! |
| COMMANDER | (*opening both hands*) Get what? Look! No gun . . . No stun ball . . . Nothing! |
| GREAT CHANG | There WAS something, Zaran. You . . . turned your hand cover. Ah! GET THE HAND COVER! |
| | (*Two* CHANGANS *take off commander's gloves and hand them to Great Chang.*) |
| CHANGA ONE | Do not move! |
| CHANGA TWO | Or you will be exterminated! |
| ALL CHANGANS | DO NOT MOVE OR YOU WILL BE EXTERMINATED! |
| GREAT CHANG | So! The Zaran has a new invention . . . an invention of small wires and tubes and a very small lens. The Changans do not know this invention. |
| | (ALL CHANGANS *move towards glove, as four* ZARAN COMMANDOS *move silently into side of arena.*) |
| | Changans! This is something we must . . . |
| COMMANDO ONE | (*shouts*) DON'T MOVE, CHANGANS! |

| | |
|---|---|
| ALL COMMANDOS | OR YOU WILL BE EXTERMINATED! |
| | (*All* CHANGANS *'freeze'.*) |
| COMMANDO ONE | Move back towards us, commander! |
| COMMANDER | (*moving back*) One blast from my humanoid ray gun, Chang, and you will be nothing more than a square metal biscuit! |
| ALL COMMANDOS | YOU WILL BE DESTROYED! |
| COMMANDER | My commandos have enough stun balls to silence a whole army of Changans. |
| ALL COMMANDOS | ALL CHANGANS WILL BE DESTROYED! |
| COMMANDER | Operate Commando Plan, Number One! |
| COMMANDO ONE | Commando Two! . . . TAKE SCANNER. Commando Three! . . . TURN EACH ONE ROUND WHEN CLEAR. |
| COMMANDO TWO | (*passing scanner over each Changan in turn*) This one's clear! And this one! |
| COMMANDO THREE | Turn round! And you! |
| COMMANDO TWO | Clear! Clear! Clear! Clear! |
| COMMANDO THREE | Round! Round! Round! Round! |
| COMMANDO ONE | Now scan Great Chang, Number Four. |
| COMMANDO FOUR | Give me the scanner, Number Two. (*He takes scanner.*) Shoulders . . . body . . . arms . . . legs! Turn round, Great Chang! |
| | (COMMANDO FOUR *stays in position, holding scanner.*) |
| COMMANDER | This round to me, Chang, thanks to my commandos. |
| COMMANDO ONE | We picked you up on the craft's long-range scanner, commander. |
| COMMANDER | Quick work! Now . . . where's my T.V. glove? |

| | |
|---|---|
| COMMANDO ONE | Over here! (*He hands glove to commander.*) |
| COMMANDER | Now to you, Great Chang. We Zarans came to Planet Changa on a peaceful mission of exploration, and we intend to leave unharmed. Do you understand? |
| GREAT CHANG | I hear your words, humanoid. |
| COMMANDER | What's the matter with you, Chang? |
| COMMANDO FOUR | (*shouts*) Something's happened! The scanner's stuck! It's stuck, commander . . . on his head! |
| COMMANDER | (*rushing forward and pulling key from underneath Great Chang's head mask*) Ah! The Great Chang's BRAIN KEY! (*He holds up key.*) |
| ALL COMMANDOS | (*in amazement*) BRAIN KEY! |
| COMMANDER | Now the Great Chang has no more brain power than his robot slaves. |
| COMMANDO ONE | So we're O.K., commander! What shall we do with the robots? |
| COMMANDER | Great Chang can program them to take no action. |
| COMMANDO TWO | What about Chang himself? |
| COMMANDER | We'll take him with us. |
| COMMANDO THREE | (*in horror*) Take him with us! What? Back to Zara? |
| COMMANDER | Back as far as the space craft. |
| COMMANDO FOUR | What shall we do with him then, commander? |
| COMMANDER | Once our ascent rockets are firing, I'll throw him his brain key. |
| COMMANDO ONE | I hope, for his sake, that he's programmed himself to put it back in the right place! |

| | |
|---|---|
| COMMANDER | Come on, Chang! Program those slaves of yours to take no action and return to their work units. |
| GREAT CHANG | Changans! TAKE NO ACTION. RETURN TO YOUR WORK UNITS. Do you understand? |
| ALL CHANGANS | WE UNDERSTAND AND OBEY! |

(CHANGANS *move out repeating.* 'We understand and obey', *as arena lights fade.*)

### END OF FIRST PLAY

# PLAYWATCHERS

*Light back on children with Space Machine.*

KAM    There's nothing on the screen.

SANDY    We've lost the picture.

JOSIE    And I wanted to see Explorer Zero Five take off.

KAM    It all seemed so real, didn't it?

SANDY    I suppose it was just a foreign T.V. channel.

JOSIE    What do you mean? That was Planet Changa! YOU think it was Planet Changa, don't you Kam?

KAM    Well . . . I thought it was when I was watching . . . but I'm not so sure now.

SANDY    Are you telling me that this (*pointing to Space Machine*) . . . CONTRAPTION, really is a SPACE MACHINE?

JOSIE    Yes I am, and if you don't believe it, you can go home.

KAM    What are you going to do with it, Josie?

JOSIE    I don't know yet . . . I might take it to . . . THE ROYAL SPACE SOCIETY!

SANDY    What! This thing! Why don't you just take it to the Science Club?

JOSIE  I might . . . but you know what grown-ups are like. They might want to keep it.

KAM  You really think that was Planet Changa, don't you Josie?

JOSIE  Yes, I do. And I'll tell you what I'm going to do now . . . I'm going to get another planet. (*She pulls the lever.*)

KAM  (*to Sandy*) You were right about Josie, you know!

SANDY  Mad!

JOSIE  Go home, then! (*laughing*) I bet you won't! (*pulling lever*) Come on, Space Machine! Come on!

(*Light comes on. Loud ticking. All three children become excited.*)

KAM  It's alive again.

SANDY  The power's back.

JOSIE  It's got universal electricity, like I said. Now, this time, let's all pull the top lever this way.

ALL CHILDREN  One . . . two . . . three . . . PULL!

(*Loud crackly voice sounds.*)

KAM  Voices!

SANDY  Say something Josie! Like you did last time.

JOSIE  (*loudly*) WHO ARE YOU? (*banging on box*) WHO ARE YOU AND WHERE DO YOU COME FROM? (*silence*) GO ON, SPACE MACHINE! SAY SOMETHING!

|       |                                                              |
|------:|--------------------------------------------------------------|
| VOICE | PLANET EARTH WILL BE DESTROYED!                              |
| KAM   | (*in horror*) Did you hear that?                             |
| SANDY | PLANET EARTH . . . that's us! We're going to be destroyed!   |
| JOSIE | It's lighting up again! LOOK!                                |
|       | (*Light fades on children.*)                                 |

*Here begins the story of* **Planet Strata.**

# Planet Strata

## Playmakers

**Stratans** – who live on Planet Strata and control the Weather Machine
TARDIS – Master of Strata and ruler of the planet
AMP – in charge of the Weather Machine
THERM ⎫
NIMBUS ⎬ weathermen, workers on the Weather Machine
ATMOS ⎭
DAY-WATCHMAN
NIGHT-WATCHMAN
FIRST WEATHER REPORTER
SECOND WEATHER REPORTER
THIRD WEATHER REPORTER
FOURTH WEATHER REPORTER

**Plasmics** – from Planet Plasma, who have come to Strata with evil intentions
KAPPA – leader of the Plasmics
ZED ⎫
GRUG ⎪
SIGMA ⎬ other Plasmics
QUEST ⎭

# Planet Strata

*The arena lights up.* THERM, NIMBUS *and* ATMOS *enter carrying a large weather chart pinned onto a screen.*

THERM (*pointing to chart*) Look at it! PLANET EARTH WILL BE DESTROYED if we send out weather like this.

NIMBUS Tardis will want an explanation.

ATMOS He's coming! The master's coming!

(*All stand behind screen as* TARDIS *enters.*)

TARDIS (*striding up to screen*) By Thunder! Planet Earth will be destroyed . . . DESTROYED . . . if Planet Strata sends out weather like this. (*banging on screen*) Explanation! Explanation!

(THERM *comes from behind screen.*)

THERM Hail, Tardis! Master of Strata!

TARDIS Temperatures for Planet Earth are out of control. (*banging on screen*) Explanation!

THERM I can't control the temperatures any more, Tardis. It's the clouds! The clouds have ruined my temperatures. Blame Nimbus. He's in charge of clouds.

(NIMBUS *hurries forward.*)

NIMBUS My clouds are out of control!

THERM They always are! You'd better do something about them, Nimbus. Your clouds are ruining all my temperatures.

NIMBUS I can't help it! I can't control them any more. Atmos can't keep the winds steady. Blame him!

(ATMOS *hurries forward.*)

| | |
|---:|:---|
| ATMOS | It's no good complaining. I can't keep the winds under control at all. The air pressure is rushing about all over the place. |
| NIMBUS | And so are my clouds! |
| ATMOS | I can't help it! I can't control the air pressure. |
| TARDIS | (*angrily*) Planet Earth will be destroyed . . . DESTROYED . . . if Planet Strata sends out weather like this. |
| THERM | Don't blame us, master! |
| NIMBUS | It's not us! |
| ATMOS | We weathermen don't CONTROL the Weather Machine. |
| WEATHERMEN | It's AMP! |
| THERM | Amp is supposed to control the Weather Machine. |
| NIMBUS | But he doesn't do it! That's the trouble! He CAN'T control it! |
| ATMOS | But he's responsible. |
| TARDIS | By Thunder! Bring Amp! |

(AMP *enters, carrying a hammer and notebook.*)

| | |
|---:|:---|
| AMP | Master! Master! I've got a problem. |
| WEATHERMEN | We know! |
| AMP | It's the Weather Machine! It's sending out terrible weather to Planet Earth. |
| WEATHERMEN | We know! |
| AMP | It's sending out WERRIBLE TEATHER . . . There! Now I'm talking like the Weather Machine. |
| THERM | What do you mean, Amp? |

AMP — (*tapping head with hammer*) I mean I'm talking back to front . . . and the Weather Machine is sending out weather which is back to front.

TARDIS — By Thunder! Planet Earth will be destroyed . . . DESTROYED . . . EXPLANATION!

AMP — (*tapping head with hammer*) I can't explain it! Everything is upside down! The seasons are back to front!

TARDIS — By Thunder! Give report!

AMP — (*consulting notebook*) Planet Earth . . . Now let me see . . . WINTER was followed by SUMMER . . . (*looking up*) They didn't get a SPRING! (*consulting notebook again*) I'm afraid they got another SUMMER . . .

TARDIS — By Thunder! Two summers and no spring! Bring the weather reporters. Bring them!

WEATHERMEN — Bring them, Amp!

AMP — Not me! I've been WEEPING out of their KAY . . . Oh dear! I've done it again! I mean, I've been keeping out of their way.

TARDIS — GO! (AMP *hurries out*) WINTER . . . SUMMER . . . SUMMER! By Thunder! If plant life on Planet Earth is destroyed then animal life will have no food . . . NO PLANTS . . . NO ANIMALS . . . NO LIFE! PLANET EARTH WILL HAVE NO LIFE!

(WEATHER REPORTERS *enter, followed by* AMP.)

ALL REPORTERS — Hail Tardis, Master of Strata!

TARDIS — Give all weather reports for Planet Earth.

FIRST REPORTER — (*reads*) Region One . . . north of equator, latitude zero to latitude 45 degrees. Sahara Desert . . . 50 centimetres of rain a day – camels up to their humps in water.

| | |
|---:|:---|
| ALL | Camels up to their humps in water! |
| AMP | In the Sahara Desert! (*groaning*) I can't believe it! |
| TARDIS | (*to reporters*) Continue report! |
| SECOND REPORTER | (*reads*) Region Two ... north of equator, latitude 45 degrees to latitude 90 degrees. Greenland ... temperature 32 degrees centigrade in the shade – igloo homes melting. |
| ALL | Igloo homes melting! |
| AMP | In Greenland! (*groaning*) I can't believe it! |
| TARDIS | (*to reporters*) Continue report! |
| THIRD REPORTER | (*reads*) Region three ... south of equator, latitude 90 degrees to latitude 45 degrees. The Antarctic ... temperature 40 degrees centigrade – penguins suffering from sunstroke. |
| ALL | Penguins suffering from sunstroke! |
| AMP | In the Antarctic! (*putting head in hands*) Dreadful! Dreadful! |
| TARDIS | (*to reporters*) Continue report! |
| FOURTH REPORTER | Region Four ... south of equator, latitude 45 degrees to latitude zero. Brazil ... snowstorms – coffee beans frozen. |
| ALL | Coffee beans frozen! |
| AMP | In Brazil! (*looking up*) It can't be true! |
| ALL REPORTERS | All weather reports correct, master. |
| | (*All look at Amp, who is tapping head with hammer.*) |
| TARDIS | (*to Amp*) By Thunder! Explanation! |
| AMP | (*springing up in excitement*) I've got it! I've got the explanation. Don't you see? The Weather Machine must be switched the WONG RAY ... I mean the WRONG WAY! |

| | |
|---:|:---|
| TARDIS | Explanation! |
| AMP | The wet regions should be dry and the dry regions wet. |
| WEATHERMEN | Wet . . . dry . . . dry . . . wet. |
| AMP | The cold regions should be hot and the COT . . . I mean HOT ones . . . should be cold. |
| WEATHERMEN | Hot . . . cold . . . cold . . . hot. |
| AMP | It's all back to front . . . like me! |
| WEATHERMEN | (*nodding*) It's back to front all right! |
| AMP | We've just got to SWITCH THE WEATHER MACHINE BACK TO FRONT! Don't you see? |
| THERM | Yes! |
| NIMBUS | Yes! |
| ATMOS | Yes! |
| AMP | Come on! |

(AMP *rushes out, followed by* TARDIS *and the* WEATHERMEN.)

| | |
|---:|:---|
| FIRST REPORTER | Everything is back to front all right! |
| SECOND REPORTER | I hope it's as simple to put right as Amp thinks. |
| THIRD REPORTER | The reports were all back to front. |
| FOURTH REPORTER | Back to front or upside down . . . we shall soon know. (*looks at own time-keeper*) We're due for the next set of reports at fourteen hundred hours. |

(REPORTERS *begin to move out as* DAY-WATCHMAN *enters.*)

| | |
|---:|:---|
| FIRST REPORTER | Here's the day-watchman. |
| DAY-WATCHMAN | Where's Amp? |
| SECOND REPORTER | He's gone to switch the Weather Machine over. |

| | |
|---|---|
| THIRD REPORTER | It isn't working properly. Amp says it's BACK TO FRONT. |
| DAY-WATCHMAN | Find Amp! It's urgent. |
| FOURTH REPORTER | Nothing could be more important than making the Weather Machine work properly. |
| DAY-WATCHMAN | Exactly! I've got GOOD NEWS. |
| ALL REPORTERS | What is it? |
| DAY-WATCHMAN | We've got visitors. |
| ALL REPORTERS | Visitors! |
| FIRST REPORTER | We're not open to visitors on Planet Strata. |
| SECOND REPORTER | Not with the Weather Machine the way it is. |
| DAY-WATCHMAN | We're open to these visitors! |
| THIRD REPORTER | Why? Who are they? |
| DAY-WATCHMAN | PLASMICS! |
| FOURTH REPORTER | PLASMICS aren't good news! |
| ALL REPORTERS | Plasmics are BAD news! |
| DAY-WATCHMAN | I know! I know! We Stratans have always tried to keep the Plasmics off our planet. But now's the time to have them on. |
| ALL REPORTERS | Why? |
| DAY-WATCHMAN | Have you forgotten that the Plasmics are skilled men? They're MACHINE MECHANICS! |
| ALL REPORTERS | MACHINE MECHANICS! Tell Amp! |
| | (*They all rush out calling,* 'Amp! Amp! Good news!') |
| DAY-WATCHMAN | I thought they'd soon realise that Plasmics are good news this time! (*He moves to side and beckons.*) This way! |
| | (*The Plasmics* KAPPA, ZED *and* GRUG *enter, carrying a tool bag.*) |

| | |
|---|---|
| KAPPA | (*looking round*) No-one here, watchman? |
| DAY-WATCHMAN | They'll be coming. |
| KAPPA | Where's the big welcome? (*turning to Zed and Grug*) For the first time in the history of the universe, we Plasmics are expecting a big welcome on Strata. Right? |
| ZED | It doesn't look like it. |
| GRUG | Where is everyone, watchman? |
| DAY-WATCHMAN | They went to switch the Weather Machine over, but . . . you all stay here. I'll fetch them myself. (*He hurries out.*) |
| KAPPA | So far, so good! SCAN! |

(ZED *and* GRUG *quickly look round arena.*)

Now! First we have to make the Stratans believe that we really have come to help them.

| | |
|---|---|
| ZED AND GRUG | Agreed! |
| KAPPA | Fortunately . . . (*laughing*) . . . they had a lot of trouble with the Weather Machine before we arrived. (*All laugh.*) |
| ZED | Thanks to me! |
| KAPPA | (*patting Zed on the back*) You did well, Zed. |
| GRUG | Didn't anyone see you when you came to Planet Strata two planet-days ago and switched the machine back to front? |
| ZED | No-one saw me. It was simple! |
| KAPPA | It was planned that way . . . a simple switch from back to front. BUT! NEXT TIME . . . |

(NIGHT-WATCHMAN *appears and watches silently from side of arena.*)

. . . next time that Weather Machine will stay out of control for six planet-months! Right?

| | |
|---|---|
| ZED AND GRUG | Right! |
| GRUG | (*pointing to tool bag*) After we've been to work with this. |
| KAPPA | Right! And remember ... These Stratans are weathermen ... They have NO WEAPONS! |
| ZED AND GRUG | (*giving thumbs up sign*) No weapons! |

(NIGHT-WATCHMAN *accidentally drops a tool and quickly disappears.*)

| | |
|---|---|
| ALL PLASMICS | What was that? |
| KAPPA | SCAN! |

(ZED *and* GRUG *quickly look round arena.*)

| | |
|---|---|
| ZED AND GRUG | No-one! |
| KAPPA | No ... when Tardis and his weathermen appear, leave the talking to me! |

(TARDIS *and* AMP *enter, followed by the* WEATHERMEN *and* DAY-WATCHMAN.)

| | |
|---|---|
| TARDIS | Greetings, Plasmics! |
| ALL STRATANS | Greetings! |
| KAPPA | Greetings! Tardis, Master of Strata! Is all well on your planet? |
| AMP | You know all isn't well, Kappa. You know that the Weather Machine is ... was ... is ... was ... is ... |
| KAPPA | Back to front? |
| TARDIS | (*quickly*) Explain how you know that. |
| KAPPA | Don't be so suspicious, Tardis. All the universe knows what your Weather Machine has been doing to Planet Earth. Besides, your day-watchman told us. |
| ZED | We've come to help you! |

| | |
|---:|:---|
| GRUG | (*pointing to tool bag*) We're skilled men. |
| AMP | (*to Tardis*) Master! The Weather Machine has been switched back to normal, but I still can't control it. Master! We must do something. |
| KAPPA | Then why not let us help you? (*looking at Tardis*) You know us, Tardis. |
| TARDIS | We know you, Kappa! |
| KAPPA | (*pretending to be angry*) We have made an offer, but if you Stratans are too proud to accept, then . . . WE'LL GO! |
| AMP | No! (*to Tardis*) We must have help, Tardis. |
| TARDIS | Planet Earth must be saved . . . we must accept. |
| AMP | (*to Plasmics*) Come with me! (AMP *and* PLASMICS *hurry out.*) I have the key! |
| TARDIS | Kappa has been known to us for many planet-years . . . He is an evil one . . . All Plasmics are evil . . . |
| THERM | We need their help, Tardis. |
| NIMBUS | And there are only three of them. |
| ATMOS | Just three cannot harm us. |
| TARDIS | Three Plasmics are three too many. |
| | (AMP *rushes in.*) |
| AMP | Master! |
| TARDIS | Why have you left the Plasmics? Where are they? |
| AMP | In the machine unit. They are checking the barometer. |
| TARDIS | Why have you left them? |
| AMP | Master! More Plasmics have arrived on Strata. |
| TARDIS | MORE? |
| ALL STRATANS | MORE? |

| | |
|---|---|
| TARDIS | How many? |
| AMP | Two more mechanics . . . and . . . some others. |
| TARDIS | (*to weathermen*) All of you! Stay with the Plasmics! Stay on full alert! |
| WEATHERMEN | We obey, Master. |
| | (AMP *and* WEATHERMEN *hurry out.*) |
| TARDIS | More Plasmics . . .! Kappa said nothing of others . . . Kappa is evil . . . (*He follows others.*) |
| | (DAY *and* NIGHT-WATCHMEN *enter, talking together.*) |
| NIGHT-WATCHMAN | I tell you, I heard those Plasmics plotting. It was quite clear. I heard the words . . . NEXT TIME . . . OUT OF CONTROL . . . |
| DAY-WATCHMAN | Is that all? |
| NIGHT-WATCHMAN | No! I heard . . . FOR SIX PLANET-MONTHS. |
| DAY-WATCHMAN | Those words could mean so many things. |
| NIGHT-WATCHMAN | They laughed together and pointed to their tool bag. They're here to do us harm. |
| DAY-WATCHMAN | But how? |
| NIGHT-WATCHMAN | I don't know. |
| DAY-WATCHMAN | You see, you don't KNOW! You're imagining things, night watchman. (*laughing*) You've watched the night stars too often. |
| NIGHT-WATCHMAN | You can laugh! Don't you think it's strange that the Plasmics should arrive just at this time? They've never offered us help before. |
| DAY-WATCHMAN | Well, they've offered it now, and we need it now. So let's hope we're getting it now. I'm off to see what's happening. (*He goes out.*) |
| NIGHT-WATCHMAN | So . . . I'm imagining things! Shall I tell Tardis now, or wait until . . .? |

(KAPPA, ZED *and* GRUG *enter.*)

KAPPA: A Stratan! Who are you, Stratan?

NIGHT-WATCHMAN: Just call me . . . Stratan!

ZED: (*menacingly*) Big Kappa asked you a friendly question.

GRUG: So, who are you? (*holding night-watchman by tunic*) We have ways of MAKING YOU TALK!

NIGHT-WATCHMAN: (*angrily*) Take your hands off me! (*pulling away*) Don't threaten me Plasmics or . . .

KAPPA: (*quickly*) It was just a joke! (*nudging Zed and Grug*) Wasn't it?

ZED: (*grinning*) Just a joke!

(*Enter* SIGMA, QUEST *and other* PLASMICS.)

NIGHT-WATCHMAN: Here are some more of your own kind. Make your jokes with them. (*He goes out.*)

SIGMA: How is it going, Big K?

KAPPA: So far, so good.

ZED: (*holding up key*) Look!

GRUG: The key to the Weather Machine unit!

QUEST: So . . . we are trusted! Good!

KAPPA: Amp gave us the key. He's the Stratan who's responsible for the machine. He trusts us.

ALL PLASMICS: (*giving 'thumbs up' sign*) Good! Good!

KAPPA: SCAN!

(PLASMICS *look round arena.*)

ZED: No-one!

GRUG: No-one!

ALL PLASMICS: No-one!

(*They gather round Kappa.*)

| | |
|---|---|
| KAPPA | Now! First we tell the Stratans that the control of the Weather Machine has a serious fault. Right? |
| ALL PLASMICS | Right! |
| KAPPA | Next we tell them that Planet Earth's weather must be switched to CONSTANT, while we carry out repairs. |
| ALL PLASMICS | CONSTANT! (*They nod to each other.*) Agreed! |

(NIGHT-WATCHMAN *moves silently to position at side.*)

| | |
|---|---|
| KAPPA | When the 'repairs' have been carried out . . . (*All laugh.*) . . . we join all controls to REVERSE. Right? |
| ALL PLASMICS | Right! ALL CONTROLS TO REVERSE! |
| KAPPA | Our masters back on Plasma have set a programme of DESTRUCTION for each separate part of the machine. |
| ZED | I like that, Big K! DESTRUCTION! |
| ALL PLASMICS | DESTRUCTION! |
| KAPPA | Here are your instructions. (*He gives each Plasmic a card, as they circle round him and raise clenched fists.*) Earth's plant life shall be destroyed! |
| ALL PLASMICS | Earth's plant life shall be destroyed! |
| KAPPA | Planet Earth shall be at our mercy! |
| ALL PLASMICS | Planet Earth shall be at our mercy! |
| KAPPA | WE SHALL RULE PLANET EARTH! |
| ALL PLASMICS | WE SHALL RULE PLANET EARTH! |
| KAPPA | (*punching air wildly*) WE SHALL BE HEROES OF PLASMA! |

| | |
|---|---|
| ALL PLASMICS | (*punching air wildly*) WE SHALL BE HEROES OF PLASMA! |
| KAPPA | GO! |
| | (PLASMICS *stride out shouting.* KAPPA *draws deep breath.*) |
| | And I shall be . . . SUPREME HERO OF PLASMA! (*He strides out.*) |
| | (NIGHT-WATCHMAN *waits, then rushes forward.*) |
| NIGHT-WATCHMAN | (*shouts*) ALERT! ALERT! |
| | (DAY-WATCHMAN *hurries in.*) |
| DAY-WATCHMAN | What now? |
| NIGHT-WATCHMAN | ALERT! ALERT! |
| | (*All* STRATANS *rush in.*) |
| TARDIS | By Thunder! What's happened? |
| NIGHT-WATCHMAN | Master! ALERT! |
| TARDIS | Report! |
| NIGHT-WATCHMAN | The Plasmics . . . have come here . . . to DESTROY . . . |
| TARDIS | TO DESTROY US! I knew it! |
| NIGHT-WATCHMAN | No, master! That is not their plan. They have come to Strata so that they can DESTROY PLANET EARTH! |
| ALL STRATANS | (*looking puzzled*) But HOW? |
| NIGHT-WATCHMAN | They will use the Weather Machine to destroy life on Planet Earth, so that they can move in and rule there themsleves. I heard them plotting . . . |
| TARDIS | By Thunder! So that is their evil plan. |

| | |
|---|---|
| NIGHT-WATCHMAN | They have gone to the Weather Machine unit to put all the controls . . . into a REVERSE position . . . and JOIN them together . . . so that they can't be moved. |
| ALL STRATANS | (*wildly*) What can we do, master? |
| TARDIS | We have time . . . The evil Plasmics cannot *enter* the Weather Machine unit. |
| AMP | (*groaning*) They can! THEY CAN! I gave them the KEY! |
| ALL STRATANS | Let's go! |
| TARDIS | Wait! If we rush them, they could destroy the Weather Machine. They have it in their power. |

(*Enter* WEATHER REPORTERS *holding a frightened* SIGMA.)

| | |
|---|---|
| SIGMA | Look! (*He holds up gloved hand with middle finger missing.*) Look! There was another finger here. (*He points to gap.*) It's GONE! |
| FIRST REPORTER | We were cleaning the instruments . . . |
| SECOND REPORTER | . . . with some solvent . . . |
| THIRD REPORTER | . . . to dissolve the rust . . . |
| FOURTH REPORTER | . . . when some of it was sprayed onto the Plasmic's hand. |
| SIGMA | (*shaking with fright*) My finger has . . . DISSOLVED! |
| TARDIS | (*holding up Sigma's hand*) Good! This is good! |
| SIGMA | (*shouts*) Good? GOOD? How can you say that? My finger has dissolved! (*in terror*) Perhaps my hand will dissolve! Perhaps I SHALL DISSOLVE! |
| TARDIS | Repeat . . . GOOD! Stratans! We can use this Plasmic. |

| | |
|---|---|
| SIGMA | (*fearfully*) USE ME? |
| TARDIS | But not yet! Take him away and keep him under guard. Yes! We can use this Plasmic. |

(SIGMA *is taken out by* FIRST *and* SECOND REPORTERS.)

| | |
|---|---|
| THERM | How, master? |
| NIMBUS | How can we use this Plasmic? |
| TARDIS | Fetch the solvent. |

(THIRD *and* FOURTH REPORTERS *go out, followed by* AMP.)

Fetch the spray guns.

| | |
|---|---|
| ATMOS | Master! What is in your mind? What will you do with the spray guns and the solvent? |

(AMP *brings in a bottle labelled 'solvent' and the spray guns.*)

| | |
|---|---|
| TARDIS | (*taking solvent*) Use it! It is a deadly weapon . . . against Plasmics! |
| THERM | (*looking puzzled*) Weapon? |
| NIMBUS | We Stratans have no weapons. |
| ATMOS | We have nothing. |
| TARDIS | Stratans have . . . a kind of weapon. |
| AMP | What is it? |
| TARDIS | These Plasmics have a . . . strange appearance. Their body coverings have a . . . peculiar touch. Now we know how to attack them. |
| AMP | But how? |
| TARDIS | The Plasmics will DISSOLVE when they are sprayed with solvent. You saw the Plasmic's finger . . . |

| | | |
|---|---|---|
| NIGHT-WATCHMAN | | (*excitedly*) You mean the finger . . . that we didn't see! (*All laugh.*) |
| | TARDIS | Exactly! Amp! The Plasmics trust you!. Bring them here. Tell them . . . Tell them that one of their group is injured . . . NOTHING MORE! |

(AMP *goes out.*)

| | |
|---|---|
| THERM | Master! What do you mean us to do? |
| TARDIS | Fill those spray guns with the solvent . . . (*All do this quickly.*) . . . and keep them at your side. |
| NIMBUS | Ah! We have weapons, at last. |
| ATMOS | Listen! (*Voices are heard.*) They're coming! Let's use our weapons. |
| TARDIS | WAIT! First Kappa must report. |

(KAPPA *enters, followed by other* PLASMICS.)

| | |
|---|---|
| KAPPA | Tardis! Where's Sigma? This Stratan . . . (*pointing to Amp*) . . . reports that he is injured. |
| TARDIS | A finger injury. It is not serious. |
| KAPPA | Where is he? |
| TARDIS | Kappa! Why have you come to Strata? Report! |
| KAPPA | We told you. |
| TARDIS | Report! Why have the Plasmics come to Strata? |
| KAPPA | What IS this? (*He looks round suspiciously.*) |
| TARDIS | WHY HAVE YOU COME TO STRATA? And why have you come AT THIS TIME? |

(STRATANS *quietly move into circle round Plasmics.*)

| | |
|---|---|
| KAPPA | Tardis! I do not like this! (*He looks round angrily.*) |
| TARDIS | By Thunder, Kappa! There is something we Stratans do not like. We Stratans do not like your evil plan. |

KAPPA   What evil plan, Stratan? We came to . . .

TARDIS   . . .FIX the Weather Machine! You came to fix the weather so that it would destroy all life on Planet Earth. Do you deny it?

ALL STRATANS   Do you deny it?

KAPPA   (*nastily*) What can you do about it, Stratan? You have no weapons.

TARDIS   (*to* AMP) Bring Sigma!

(AMP *goes out.*)

See for yourself Kappa! By Thunder! See what we Stratans can do without weapons.

KAPPA   Without weapons . . . you can do nothing.

(AMP, REPORTERS *and other* STRATANS *enter with* SIGMA.)

ALL STRATANS   Sigma is here, master.

SIGMA   Plasmics! Kappa! These Stratans have a weapon.

KAPPA   (*in surprise*) A weapon! What is it?

SIGMA   (*holding up hand with missing finger*) Look at my hand!

ZED   (*in amazement*) Look at his hand!

GRUG   The middle finger's missing!

QUEST   (*looking closely*) It's . . . It's . . . disappeared!

KAPPA   (*narrowing eyes*) But HOW? What have you Stratans done?

TARDIS   We have a secret weapon, Kappa. Stratans! On guard!

(ALL STRATANS *hold out spray guns in two-handed grip.*)

You see!

KAPPA (*scornfully*) SPRAY GUNS!

TARDIS You jeer, Kappa! By Thunder! You are a fool! Each spray gun holds the solvent which will slowly dissolve all your plasmic body coverings.

KAPPA I don't believe it!

SIGMA (*angrily*) You CAN believe it, Kappa!

TARDIS Your skin is not like that of other planet dwellers, Kappa. I have known that for some time.

KAPPA (*beginning to look worried*) That's not so ... No!

SIGMA Yes, Kappa! (*looking at hand*) You can believe it! (*in horror*) Look! My next finger is beginning to ... dissolve!

KAPPA (*signalling to Plasmics to close up*) You won't do it, Tardis.

TARDIS By Thunder! We'll do it, Kappa! STRATANS! ALERT! READY TO FIRE!

KAPPA PLASMICS! RETREAT! (*yells*) RUN!

TARDIS FIRE!

(PLASMICS *turn and run off, shouting wildly.* STRATANS *follow, calling after them and spraying them with solvent. Arena lights fade. Screen is carried out.*)

## END OF SECOND PLAY

 # PLAYWATCHERS

*Light back on children with Space Machine.*

KAM — Oh no! It's gone! They've all gone!

SANDY — We've lost them. Just as the Stratans were going to make those Plasmics dissolve before our very eyes.

JOSIE — So you both believe it then?

KAM — I believe it!

SANDY — I'm beginning to . . . After all, we did SEE it happen!

JOSIE — But will other people believe us?

KAM — We can tell them that we've seen TWO different planets.

SANDY — They could still say it was another foreign T.V. channel.

JOSIE — Well . . . we can try once more. If we can get THREE different planets, they'll HAVE to believe us.

SANDY — Try it again, Josie.

JOSIE — Come on, Space Machine! (*pulling lever*) Come alive again!

(*Lights come on. Loud ticking. The children become excited.*)

KAM — Alive!

SANDY   There's plenty of universal electricity!

JOSIE   Now, let's pull the lever another way this time. This way ... Ready ...!

ALL   One ... two ... three ... PULL!

(*Loud crackly voice sounds.*)

KAM   Voices!

SANDY   Go on, Josie!

JOSIE   (*loudly*) WHO ARE YOU? (*banging on box*) WHO ARE YOU AND WHERE DO YOU COME FROM? Go on, Space Machine. TALK!

VOICE   EXTERMINATE THEM! EXTERMINATE THEM!

KAM   (*excitedly*) We're there again!

SANDY   I wonder who's going to be exterminated?

JOSIE   We shall soon know! Look!

(*Light fades on children.*)

*Here begins the story of* Planet Crysta.

# Planet Crysta

## Playmakers

**Crystans** – who live on the crystal Planet Crysta
CRYSTAL QUEEN – ruler of the planet
OPAL – her adviser

ALPHA ⎤
BETA  ⎥
GAMMA ⎬ Crystan spies
DELTA ⎦

EDAL   ⎤
ASTRAL ⎥
DIAD   ⎬ Crystan slaves
GRAINE ⎦

**Spargans** – visitors from Planet Spar
SILVERA – leader of the Spargans
CALLUM – his first lieutenant

AXEL ⎤
ALUM ⎬ Spargan crystal collectors
ASH  ⎦

MICRO ⎤
CHIP  ⎦ two Spargans on their first crystal collecting expedition

Other Spargans

# Planet Crysta

*The arena lights up. The* CRYSTAL QUEEN *storms angrily in, followed by* OPAL.

CRYSTAL QUEEN: The strangers must be exterminated! Exterminate them! Exterminate them, I say!

OPAL: Not yet, O Shining One!

CRYSTAL QUEEN: Why do you say, NOT YET? These strangers have come to Planet Crysta to steal our crystal gems. Exterminate them!

OPAL: Later perhaps, O Shining One. But not yet.

CRYSTAL QUEEN: (*impatiently*) Why not, Opal? Why not? Tell me why we should not exterminate these . . . these . . . THIEVES!

OPAL: Shining One! Our spies say that these strangers carry . . . SECRETS!

CRYSTAL QUEEN: Secrets! What secrets?

OPAL: CRYSTAL secrets.

CRYSTAL QUEEN: Bah! We Crystans have all crystal secrets, Opal.

OPAL: We Crystans cannot make our own crystal gems, Shining One. We cannot MAKE CRYSTALS.

CRYSTAL QUEEN: Bah! Crystals cannot be MADE. All crystal gems must be cut from the granite rocks . . . OUR granite rocks.

OPAL: Your spies have heard these strangers talk of making . . . COLOURED CRYSTALS!

CRYSTAL QUEEN: COLOURED CRYSTALS!

OPAL: Shining One! You have always wanted COLOURED crystals. There are none here on Planet Crysta.

| | |
|---|---|
| CRYSTAL QUEEN | We have you, Opal! (*looking at him closely*) You are not bright and you do not sparkle, but you have a little colour. You are . . . better than nothing. |
| OPAL | Perhaps these strangers can make crystal gems that are as bright and sparkling as you, O Queen . . . but also COLOURED. |
| CRYSTAL QUEEN | COLOURED CRYSTALS! Mmm! Bring my spies! |
| OPAL | (*moving quickly to side of arena and calling*) You have been summoned! Come! |

(*Enter four* CRYSTAN SPIES.)

| | |
|---|---|
| ALL SPIES | (*bowing*)<br>Hail to the Brightness!<br>Hail to the Light!<br>Hail to the Shining One! |
| CRYSTAL QUEEN | (*to spies*) What do you know? |
| ALPHA | Strangers have come to Crysta, O Shining One. |
| CRYSTAL QUEEN | Who are they? |
| BETA | Spargans! They have come from Planet Spar. |
| CRYSTAL QUEEN | Spargans! Spargans have colours! What are their colours? |
| GAMMA | All colours, Shining One. |
| DELTA | They are brighter than Opal. They are very clear. |
| CRYSTAL QUEEN | There are no crystal rocks on Spar. (*mutters*) They must be thieves! I feel it in my crystals! (*to spies*) But . . . Where are they now? |
| ALPHA | They are searching amongst the salt flats and rocks for crystals. |
| BETA | I heard them talk of growing COLOURED crystal gems from crystal seeds. |

| | |
|---|---|
| CRYSTAL QUEEN | COLOURED crystals! But if they can grow their own crystal gems, why should they come to Planet Crysta? Tell me that. |
| GAMMA | They are looking for some special kind of crystal. |
| DELTA | We heard them talk of . . . QUARTZ! |
| CRYSTAL QUEEN | (*angrily*) QUARTZ! They know about our crystal quartz! They've come to rob us. They must be EX . . . |
| OPAL | (*interrupting*) Wait, Shining One! We must know more before we act. |
| CRYSTAL QUEEN | (*impatiently*) How, Opal? How? |
| OPAL | These spies must be our ears and eyes. (*to Queen*) Come, Shining One. We will go into the Hexagon. (*to spies*) Learn the Spargans' secrets and you will be well rewarded. |
| | (CRYSTAL QUEEN *and* OPAL *go out*.) |
| ALPHA | We must become faceless. This is how we'll learn. Listen! (*Voices are heard*.) Someone is coming now. |
| BETA | I'll scan! |
| GAMMA | And I. (*They run to side of arena*.) |
| BETA | Spargans! And they're coming this way. |
| GAMMA | There are three! |
| ALPHA | We'll listen to their talk and learn their secrets. We'll watch from here. |
| | (SPIES *move to side as* AXEL, ALUM *and* ASH *enter*.) |
| AXEL | (*licking lips*) Salt! Salt! Salt! You can taste it everywhere. |
| ALUM | (*rubbing eyes*) It's in my eyes . . . it's up my nose . . . it's in my ears . . . it's everywhere. |

ASH  (*holding up grain of salt between fingers*) These grains of salt are too small to see . . . I hope we shall find crystals bigger than these.

AXEL  I'd like to find a crystal as big as my head.

ALUM  (*laughing*) Nothing comes as big as that, Axel!

ASH  Silvera has to get his hands on the real stuff for our radio men.

AXEL  We've got to find QUARTZ.

ALUM  REAL . . . QUARTZ.

ASH  When we've found pure quartz, we can build the greatest radio network in the universe.

AXEL  It's strange. There's no sign of a radio network on this planet.

ALUM  (*tapping head*) These Crystans haven't got the know-how.

ASH  And we haven't got the quartz we need! (*taking out map*) Let's look at the map.

AXEL  (*pointing*) We came this way . . .

ALUM  . . . over these salt flats . . . and between these rocks.

ASH  Silvera and Callum were to come through the caves . . . (*pointing*) here . . . and the new men were to climb these rocks . . . (*pointing*) here.

AXEL  Ah! The new men! Micro and Chip! What do you think of them?

ALUM  I'm not sure . . . yet.

ASH  I don't trust them. I don't know why.

AXEL  They're up to something! Have you noticed how often they stop their conversation when one of us moves close enough to hear what they are saying?

ALUM  Silvera seems to trust them.

ASH     Silvera trusts everyone!

AXEL     Silvera can only think of one thing on this expedition ...

ALUM, ASH     Quartz!

AXEL     (*spreading out map on ground*) Let's look again ... (*All kneel and study map with backs to spies.*) .... Here are the Granite Rocks ...

(MICRO *and* CHIP *creep in and watch from hiding place.*)

... There should be pure crystals here. (*He jabs at map.*)

(*On signal from* ALPHA, SPIES *move forward and overcome Spargans from behind.*)

ALPHA     (*pointing ray gun*) Do not move, Spargans! Do not move, or you will be exterminated!

BETA     (*pushing Axel face down on ground*) Spargan One ... immobilised!

GAMMA     (*pushing Alum down*) Spargan Two ... immobilised!

DELTA     (*pushing Ash down*) Spargan Three ... immobilised!

ALPHA     Scan the prisoners for weapons.

BETA     (*passing scanner over Axel*) Ah! There is a metal object ... in here. (*taking rock chipper from Axel's pocket*) A rock chipper ... NO WEAPONS!

GAMMA     (*passing scanner over Alum*) Metal! (*taking rock hammer from Alum's pocket*) A rock hammer ... NO WEAPONS!

DELTA     (*passing scanner over Ash*) Metal! (*taking rock knife from Ash's pocket*) A rock knife ... NO WEAPONS!

| | |
|---:|:---|
| ALPHA | Up! Up! Up! |
| | (*The* SPARGANS *get up.*) |
| AXEL | Now you know that we came on a peaceful mission . . . |
| ALUM | . . . to look for crystals. |
| ALPHA | THIEVES! SPARGAN THIEVES! |
| ASH | We're not thieves! When our leader, Silvera, comes . . . |
| ALPHA | (*interrupting*) Ah! You have a leader! You can tell your story to our Crystal Queen. |
| AXEL | Willingly but . . . |
| ALPHA | Keep these Spargans under close guard. We'll take them to our Queen. |
| | (SPARGANS *are taken out by* CRYSTANS. MICRO *comes forward and beckons* CHIP.) |
| MICRO | (*laughing*) They've gone! Those fools asked for trouble! |
| CHIP | (*pointing at map with thumb*) They even had the map out! |
| MICRO | (*laughing*) They were soon immobilised! The Advance Information Service reported that these Crystans have no weapons except for simple ray guns. |
| CHIP | (*patting pocket*) Nothing like this fellow here! |
| MICRO | It's amazing! Crystans have nothing except simple ray guns to protect pure crystal quartz. |
| CHIP | Let's hope they won't have so much when we've been to work here! |
| MICRO | Not so fast, Chip! We're a long way from getting our hands on it. |
| CHIP | We'll get it, Micro! Silvera will lead us to it . . . and then we'll get our hands on it. |

MICRO  (*holding up hand*) Listen! SCAN! (*They look round.*) Take cover! (*They return to hiding place.*)

(SILVERA, CALLUM *carrying crystal box and the other* SPARGANS *enter.*)

CALLUM  That's strange! I could have sworn I heard voices.

SILVERA  SCAN!

(SPARGANS *scan area.* CALLUM *finds Micro and Chip.*)

CALLUM  Ah! Micro! Chip! Anything to report?

MICRO  Plenty!

SILVERA  (*excitedly*) Have you found QUARTZ?

MICRO  We haven't found anything, Silvera, but we've lost some Spargans.

CALLUM  Who? What do you mean?

SILVERA  Where are Axel and the others? REPORT!

MICRO  They've been taken for questioning.

SILVERA  REPORT!

MICRO  Caught . . . with their tools and map out here . . . Said they were looking for quartz . . . Accused of thieving . . . Taken away.

CALLUM  Trouble? How much trouble was there?

CHIP  Trouble! Plenty for Axel!

CALLUM  Was there real trouble?

CHIP  They gave in . . . No guns out, if that's what you mean.

SILVERA  The sooner we can make contact with the Crystan leader, the better. Advance Information Service reported that these Crystans had a Crystal Queen . . .

| | |
|---|---|
| CALLUM | . . . and some kind of adviser . . . an . . . Opal. |
| | (OPAL *enters with other* CRYSTANS, *who form a ring round Spargans.*) |
| OPAL | I am Opal. Advance Information Service has served you well. |
| SILVERA | Hail, Opal! We came in friendship, but you have taken three Spargans. Where is your queen? Where is your leader? |
| OPAL | The Crystal Queen comes! |
| | (CRYSTAL QUEEN *enters, with four* CRYSTAN SLAVES.) |
| ALL SLAVES | (*bowing*) Hail to the Brightness! Hail to the Light! Hail to the Shining One! |
| SILVERA | Hail to the Brightness! |
| CALLUM | Hail to the Light! |
| ALL SPARGANS | Hail to the Shining One! |
| SILVERA | Queen! I am leader of the Spargans. |
| CRYSTAL QUEEN | We know who you are, Silvera. |
| SILVERA | We have come to Planet Crysta on a peaceful mission. |
| CRYSTAL QUEEN | You came to steal our quartz, Silvera! (*angrily*) You are thieves! |
| SILVERA | We are not thieves. We are crystal collectors and we will bargain with you for . . . |
| CRYSTAL QUEEN | (*interrupting*) We have three of your Spargans, Silvera. |
| SILVERA | My Spargans did no harm and . . . |
| CRYSTAL QUEEN | Tell us something, Silvera . . . |
| SILVERA | Tell you what, Queen? |

| | |
|---|---|
| CRYSTAL QUEEN | Tell us . . . YOUR SECRETS! |
| SILVERA | (*in surprise*) We have no secrets, Shining One. (*turning to Spargans*) What secrets have we, Spargans? |
| ALL SPARGANS | None! We have no secrets. |
| | (MICRO *and* CHIP *slip out quietly and unnoticed.*) |
| CRYSTAL QUEEN | (*angrily*) You have secrets, Silvera. |
| OPAL | Our spies have heard talk of how you Spargans grow coloured crystal gems from seeds . . . in water jars. How do you do it? |
| SILVERA | Ah! (*looking carefully at Crystans*) COLOURED crystal gems! Perhaps it would be to your advantage and to ours, if we exchanged some of our coloured crystal gems for . . . for . . . |
| CRYSTAL QUEEN | We know you want our crystal quartz, Silvera. |
| CALLUM | It's for our radio network, back on Spar. We plan to send radio messages over all our planet, but to do it we must have pure crystal quartz. |
| CRYSTAL QUEEN | Bah! I knew it! You want our quartz. |
| SILVERA | You want our secrets, Queen. |
| OPAL | (*quickly*) Let's make a bargain with these Spargans, Shining One. |
| SILVERA | (*quickly*) When the Spargans you have taken are returned to us, unharmed, we can start talking. |
| CRYSTAL QUEEN | Slaves! Come forward! |
| ALL SLAVES | We are at your command, O Shining One. |
| CRYSTAL QUEEN | Bring the Spargans to us. |
| ALL SLAVES | We obey your command, O Shining One. |
| | (SLAVES *go out.*) |
| CRYSTAL QUEEN | Now let us learn your secrets, Silvera. |

| | |
|---:|:---|
| SILVERA | When the Spargans are here . . . unharmed. |
| | (*Enter* SLAVES.) |
| ALL SLAVES | The Spargans come, O Shining One. |
| | (SPIES *bring in* SPARGANS.) |
| AXEL | We are unharmed, Silvera. |
| ALUM | Silvera! Where are the others? |
| ASH | (*looking round*) Where are Micro and Chip? |
| CALLUM | (*looking round*) They were here . . . Micro and Chip are missing. |
| OPAL | SEARCH! |
| | (SPIES *rush out.*) |
| | Silvera! Where are your thieves? |
| SILVERA | I have no knowledge. |
| OPAL | So you say, Silvera. |
| CRYSTAL QUEEN | (*angrily*) These Spargans are thieves. I feel it in my crystals! Exterminate them! Exterminate them, I say. |
| | (SPIES *return with* MICRO *and* CHIP, *and fling them to the ground.*) |
| OPAL | REPORT! |
| ALPHA | These Spargans had reached the Inner Room. |
| BETA | They were moving towards the Hexagon! |
| ALL CRYSTANS | THE HEXAGON! |
| GAMMA | This Spargan (*pointing to Micro*) . . . had a quartz crystal in his hand. |
| DELTA | And this one (*pointing to Chip*) . . . had rock tools. |
| CRYSTAL QUEEN | (*furiously*) THIEVES! They are all thieves! These Spargans came to steal our crystal quartz. They must be exterminated! |

|  |  |
|---|---|
|  | (SPIES *and* SLAVES *make a circle round the Spargans.*) |
| OPAL | Wait, O Shining One! (*cunningly*) This Silvera has crystals in many colours. Why not spare his life in exchange for coloured crystals? |
| SILVERA | (*on knees*) Spare us all, O Shining One. Spare us all and you will be rewarded. (*to Spargans*) PLEAD! |
| ALL SPARGANS | (*on knees*) Spare us, O Shining One. |
| OPAL | It is to our advantage, Shining One. |
| CRYSTAL QUEEN | Very well! I will spare Silvera . . . in exchange for . . . coloured crystals. |
| SILVERA | (*standing up*) ALL of us, O Shining One! (*quietly*) Think! Dead Spargans cannot make coloured crystals. |
|  | (SPARGANS *stand up and* SILVERA *points to Micro and Chip*) |
|  | These two will be punished by the Spargan court. |
| OPAL | Consider it, Queen. As Silvera says, DEAD SPARGANS CANNOT MAKE COLOURED CRYSTALS. |
| SILVERA | You have quartz crystals . . . we have coloured ones. Let's exchange our gifts. |
| OPAL | There is good sense in this, O Shining One. |
| SILVERA | (*cunningly*) A bright necklace of many coloured crystals, such as the Spargans grow in water jars, would look well . . . around your neck, Queen. |
| CALLUM | (*moving forward*) There would be coloured crystal necklets for your slaves . . . |
| OPAL | Consider it, O Shining One. (*He signals to slaves.*) |
| ALL SLAVES | Consider it, O Shining One. |

| | |
|---|---|
| CALLUM | There would be pale green and blue . . . purple . . . and yellow crystals. |
| EDAL | Pale green! |
| ASTRAL | And blue! |
| DIAD | Purple! |
| GRAINE | And yellow! |
| CRYSTAL QUEEN | Let me . . . let me . . . let me SEE the crystals. |
| CALLUM | (*taking crystals from crystal box*) Pale green . . . blue . . . purple . . . yellow. |
| ALL CRYSTANS | (*pleading*) Pale green . . . blue . . . purple . . . yellow. COLOURED crystals, O Shining One. |
| CRYSTAL QUEEN | We'll have them, Silvera, and you can have your thieves. Take them with you back to Spar. |
| SILVERA | We'll take them and some quartz, O Shining One. We must have crystal quartz. We cannot return without it. |
| CRYSTAL QUEEN | Silvera! You want too much. |
| OPAL | (*quickly*) Wait, Shining One. These Spargans still have their secret. We must know how to make coloured crystals for ourselves. |
| SILVERA | (*taking four packets from crystal box*) For these secrets, we must have pure quartz. |
| OPAL | Show us! |
| CALLUM | (*holding up packet labelled* NICKEL SULPHATE) This one . . . will give you GREEN. (*holding up packet labelled* COPPER SULPHATE) This . . . BLUE. (*holding up packet labelled* CHROME ALUM) For PURPLE, you need this. (*holding up packet labelled* POTASSIUM CHROMATE) And this . . . for YELLOW. |
| CRYSTAL QUEEN | (*greedily*) We'll take them, Spargan. |

| | |
|---:|:---|
| SILVERA | (*pushing Callum back*) And we'll take QUARTZ! |
| CRYSTAL QUEEN | I'll, give you quartz if . . . |
| ALL SPARGANS | (*excitedly*) QUARTZ! QUARTZ! |
| CRYSTAL QUEEN | (*holding up hand*) If . . . IF . . . you can win it from me, Silvera. |
| SILVERA | Win it? What do you mean? |
| CRYSTAL QUEEN | Slaves! |
| ALL SLAVES | We are at your command, O Shining One. |
| CRYSTAL QUEEN | Bring me my 'magic square' board. |
| ALL SLAVES | We obey your command, O Queen. |
| | (SLAVES *go out*.) |
| CALLUM | (*to Opal*) What is this magic square board? |
| OPAL | A contest which our Queen favours. |
| CALLUM | A contest! Is it one of skill? |
| OPAL | One of great skill, Spargan. You will see. |
| | (SLAVES *bring in and set up a large 'magic square' board, with four numbers missing.*) |
| SILVERA | What is the challenge? |
| OPAL | You must find the missing numbers. |
| CALLUM | (*whispers*) Silvera! Play for quartz! |
| SILVERA | I'll play for QUARTZ! |
| CRYSTAL QUEEN | I knew it! |
| OPAL | (*pointing to board*) The sum of each horizontal (*drawing line in air with finger*), the sum of each vertical (*drawing another line*), and the sum of each diagonal (*drawing another line*) are THE SAME. |

|   |   |   |
|---|---|---|
| 4 | 9 | 2 |
|   |   |   |
| 8 |   | 6 |

| ALL SPARGANS | (*clapping hands together*) The sum of each horizontal, the sum of each vertical and the sum of each diagonal are THE SAME! GO ON, SILVERA! (*They push him forward.*) |
|---|---|
| OPAL | You have just twenty planet-seconds, Silvera! SLAVES! |
| ALL SLAVES | (*swaying rhythmically as they count*) One . . . Two . . . Three . . . |
| OPAL | (*interrupting*) WAIT! Silvera! Here are your numbers. You must find the four missing numbers and you must give the totals.<br><br>(SILVERA *takes the cards with the numbers on them. He moves to board.*)<br><br>Slaves! Begin your count again . . . NOW! |
| ALL SLAVES | One . . . Two . . . Three . . . (*They continue quietly counting.*) |
| SILVERA | (*glancing at hand calculator and putting numbers on board*) This one is ONE! This one . . . THREE! (*glancing at calculator again*) This one is . . . FIVE. (*glancing at calculator*) And this one . . . SEVEN. (*moving fingers along board and speaking quickly*) The sum of the horizontals, the sum of the verticals and the sum of the diagonals is fifteen. (*turning round*) DONE! |
| ALL SLAVES | (*counting loudly*) NINE . . . TEN . . . |
| OPAL | STOP, Slaves! (*in amazement*) How did you do it Silvera? Ah! There is something in your hand. What is it? |
| SILVERA | (*putting hand behind back*) A Spargan secret! |
| CRYSTAL QUEEN | (*greedily*) What is it, Silvera? |
| SILVERA | (*holding out calculator*) A calculator. |
| CRYSTAL QUEEN | (*greedily*) I want it! |

```
4 9 2
3 5 7
8 1 6
```

| | |
|---:|:---|
| SILVERA | No! (*putting hand behind back*) You challenged me for . . . QUARTZ! I have won, so keep your word. |
| CRYSTAL QUEEN | Slaves! Bring the quartz. |
| ALL SLAVES | We obey your command, O Queen. (*They go out.*) |
| CRYSTAL QUEEN | So, you have won, Silvera. |
| SILVERA | And you will keep your word, O Shining One. |
| | (SLAVES *enter, carrying a tray of crystal quartz.*) |
| ALL SPARGANS | CRYSTAL QUARTZ! |
| CALLUM | Opal! (*handing over crystal box*) Take these! |
| OPAL | Here is your quartz, Spargan. |
| | (CALLUM *takes the tray.*) |
| CRYSTAL QUEEN | Silvera . . . |
| SILVERA | (*holding up calculator*) I listen, O Queen. |
| CRYSTAL QUEEN | Silvera, let me hold your calculator in my hand. |
| | (SILVERA *places calculator in Queen's hand.*) |
| OPAL | Shining One! (*whispers loudly*) There is a . . . GREAT crystal quartz! |
| | (CRYSTAL QUEEN *nods and* OPAL *goes out.*) |
| SILVERA | A GREAT crystal quartz? |
| CRYSTAL QUEEN | We keep our treasures in the Hexagon. (*pointing to Micro and Chip*) These thieves must have known of it. |
| | (OPAL *enters, carrying large crystal.*) |
| ALL SPARGANS | (*in amazement*) OH! |
| CRYSTAL QUEEN | This great crystal quartz would be a fair exchange for . . . A CALCULATOR . . . I think! |
| SILVERA | Agreed! (*They exchange calculator for quartz.*) |
| | (SPARGANS *and* CRYSTANS *go out applauding.*) |

# END OF THIRD PLAY

 # PLAYWATCHERS

*Light on children with Space Machine.*

KAM    I knew it would end like that.

SANDY    I wish I had the crystal box. I'd like to make crystals.

JOSIE    You could you know. It's easy!

KAM    I'd like to go to the Planet Crysta.

SANDY    I wonder what happened to Micro and Chip.

JOSIE    We'd better decide what's going to happen to our Space Machine. I think we'd better take it to the Space Society.

KAM    Will they believe us?

SANDY    They'll have to. We can describe three different planets. They'll have to!

JOSIE    (*to Sandy*) So you believe it?

SANDY    Of course I do.

JOSIE    We shall have to try and give them a demonstration. Remember, the lever goes north to Planet Changa . . . (*She pulls lever.*)

(*Arena lights up. Enter all characters in 'Planet Changa'.*)

| | |
|---|---|
| ALL CHARACTERS | Here we are! We've answered your call, <br> Give a clap or a whistle – or nothing at all. <br> North, south, east, west, <br> Changa! Changa! Changa's best! |
| JOSIE | And south to Planet Strata . . . (*She pulls lever.*) |
| | (*Enter all characters in 'Planet Strata'.*) |
| ALL CHARACTERS | (*as they cross arena and go out*) <br> Here we are! We've answered your call, <br> Give a clap or a whistle – or nothing at all. <br> North, south, east, west, <br> Strata! Strata! Strata's best! |
| JOSIE | And east to Planet Crysta . . . (*She pulls lever.*) |
| | (*Enter all characters in 'Planet Crysta'.*) |
| ALL CHARACTERS | (*as they cross arena and go out*) <br> Here we are! We've answered your call, <br> Give a clap or a whistle – or nothing at all. <br> North, south, east, west, <br> Crysta! Crysta! Crysta's best! |
| ALL CHILDREN | North! South! East! West! <br> We've decided – EARTH'S BEST! |
| | (*They pick up the Space Machine and go out repeating:* North! South! *etc.*) |

# Suggestions for the Playmakers

If you are a character from another planet you can wear a loose tunic. Cut out a sign to show which planet you come from. Here are some suggestions.

 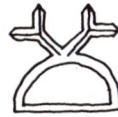    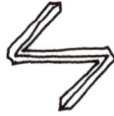

Zaran    Changan    Stratan    Plasmic    Crystan    Spargan

Hands can be covered with gloves, mittens or socks.
Knee socks can be pulled over jeans.
Heavy boots or track shoes can be worn and legs bandaged with strips of material. Boots can be made from two pieces of foam rubber, stitched together.

The Plasmics in 'Planet Strata' can wear rubber gloves, with rubber bands round the wrists. Sigma will need a rubber glove with a string 'puller' attached to one finger. With the finger out of the glove finger, pull the string to 'dissolve' it.

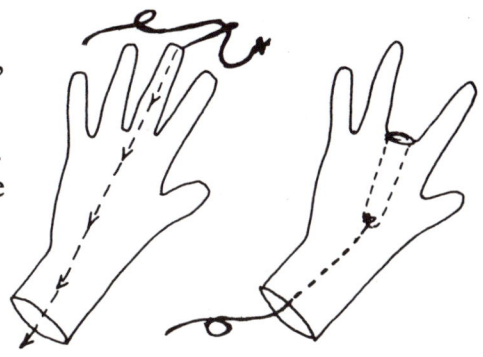

Make a head-dress for the Crystal Queen in 'Planet Crysta'.

1 Cut out the shape from a strong piece of cardboard.
2 Bend lengths of wire with hook shapes at the top. Fasten these securely inside the crown with strong adhesive tape.
3 Bend the crown into a circular shape and fasten it securely at the back. Cover it with silver foil and hang beads on the wire hooks as crystals.

Make different masks for the characters from the different planets.
Make a simple mask from felt or thin card. Practise first with newspaper. Fold the material in half. Cut it to shape and cut out eye holes.
Attach strings or elastic for fastening it round your head. Decorate it.

Make cylindrical masks from thin cardboard for the robots in 'Planet Changa' to drop over their heads.
Fasten securely at the back, cut holes for eyes, nose and mouth, then decorate. You can also make paper bag or sack masks. Cut out eye and mouth holes. Stick on strips of paper or string for hair, then decorate.

If you are a Zaran in 'Planet Changa' you could pull a stocking mask over your head. Mark the positions of the eyes, nose and mouth. Smear adhesive round the marks to prevent the stocking from running. Allow this to dry before cutting out shapes. You can tie the foot of the stocking at the top, to make a pigtail. Decorate the mask.

To make a quartz crystal for 'Planet Crysta' trace the diagram onto thin card, and cut out the shape. Fold along the dotted lines. Glue the flap and stick it under the opposite end. Stick the points together with adhesive tape. Cover the crystal with coloured foil.

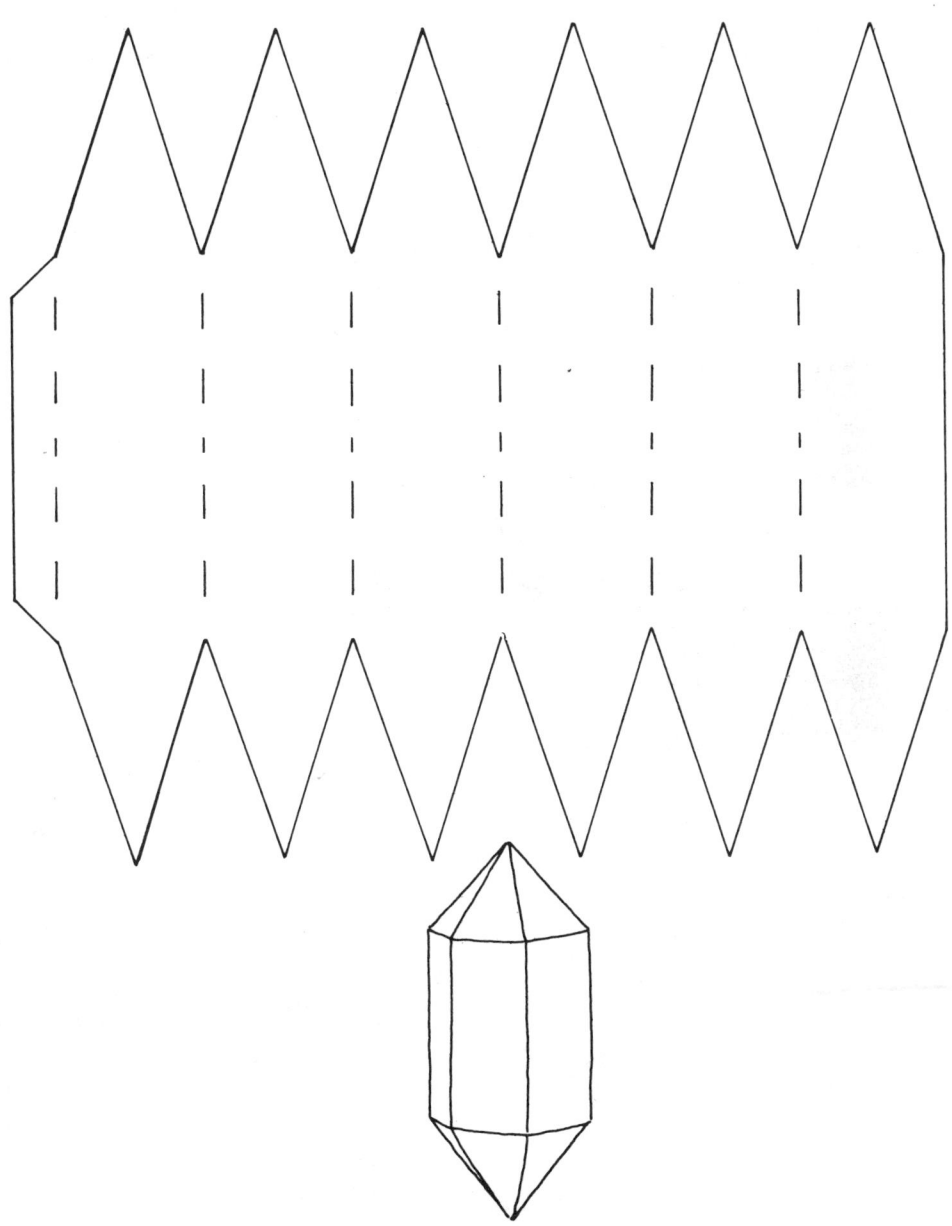

## Props

Use a large cardboard box for the Space Machine. Cut out a rectangle for the screen at the front and cover it with cling film. Cut narrow slots for the levers, as shown in the diagram. Levers can be made from strips of wood.

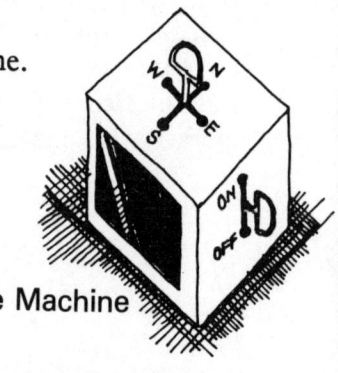

Space Machine

Borrow a dinner or library trolley for the truth machine in 'Planet Changa'. Fit a box on top with possibly a portable T.V. aerial. Old handle bars from bicycles can be added at each end, or handles can be made from cardboard cylinders covered with foil.

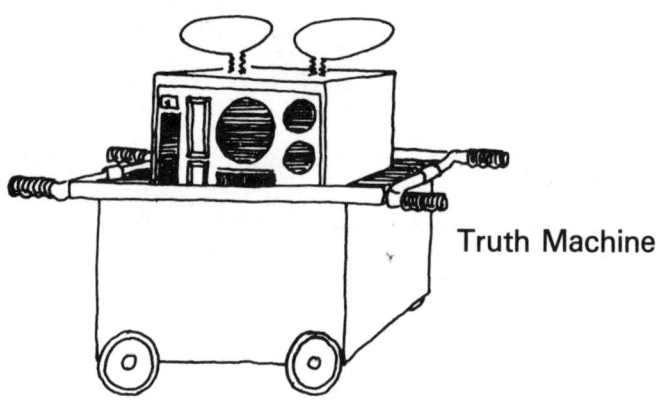

Truth Machine

Use a torch for the scanner in 'Planet Changa' and 'Planet Crysta'. Use small plant or laundry spray bottles filled with water for the spray guns in 'Planet Strata'.